GNOME sweet GNOME

Kids Magical Baking

by the editors of Klutz

D1214925

KLUTZ

contents

CAKES

COOKIES

CHOCOLATE

BREADS

PIES & CRUSTS

POTIONS

what you get

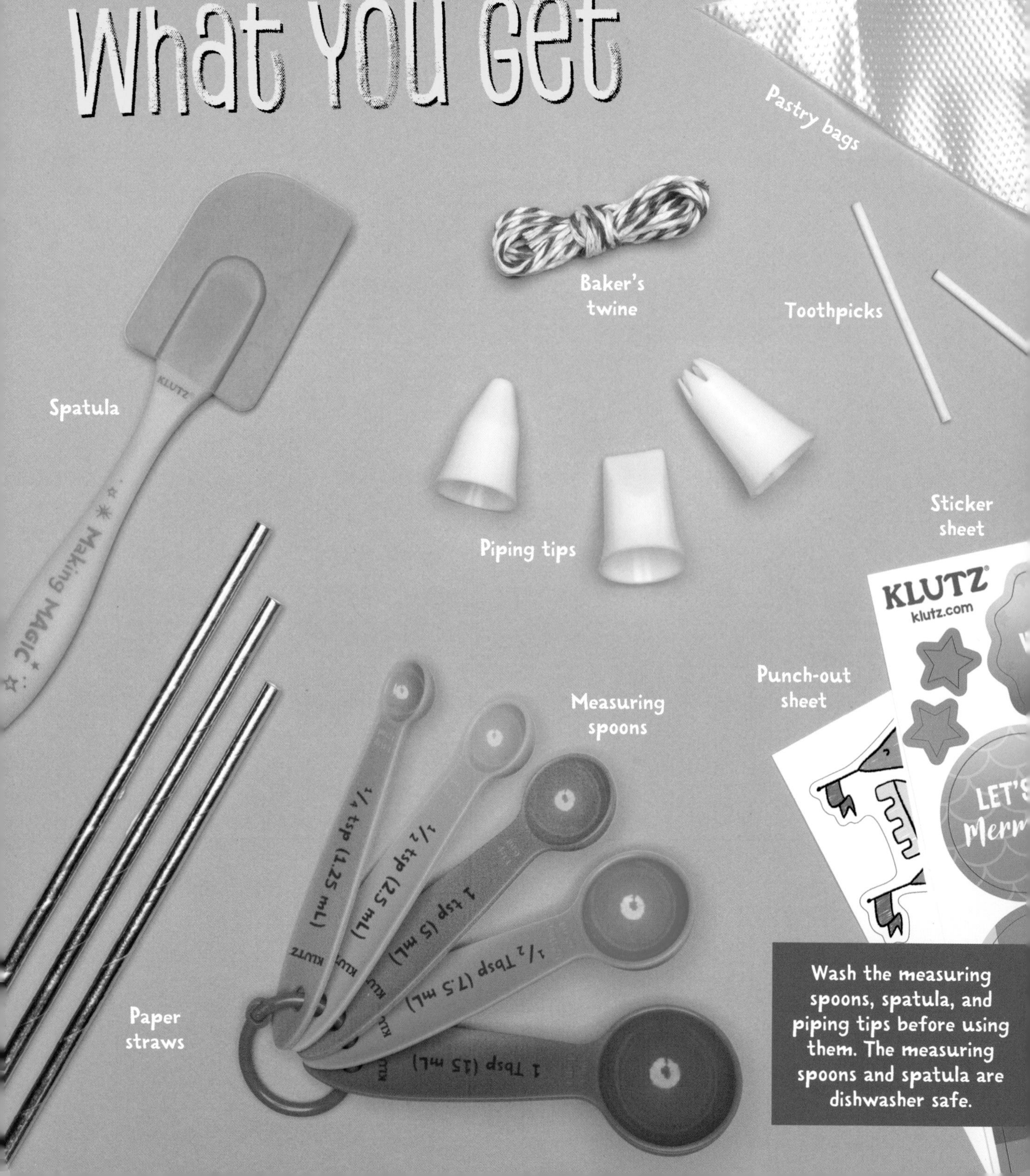

Pastry bags

Baker's twine

Toothpicks

Spatula

KLUTZ

Making Magic

Piping tips

Sticker sheet

Punch-out sheet

KLUTZ®
klutz.com

LET'S
Merm

Measuring spoons

Paper straws

1/4 tsp (1.25 mL)

1/2 tsp (2.5 mL)

1 tsp (5 mL)

1/2 Tbsp (7.5 mL)

1 Tbsp (15 mL)

KLUTZ

Wash the measuring spoons, spatula, and piping tips before using them. The measuring spoons and spatula are dishwasher safe.

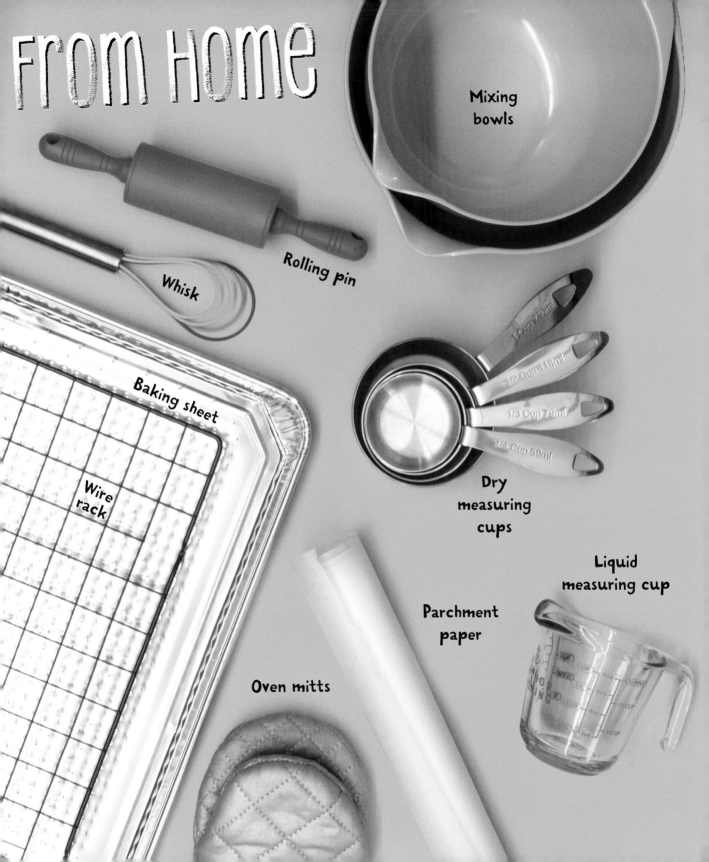

The Kitchen Rules!

We here at Klutz believe that the kitchen is a very special room in your house, with special rules.

1. Be careful! The kid chef should talk with their grown-up assistant about any recipe ahead of time. If the recipe calls for a knife, a hot stove, or an oven, the grown-up assistant should always do those tasks. Use the grown-up's judgment when the kid chef is ready to take on more responsibility in the kitchen. Oh, and it's not a bad idea to have a fire extinguisher on hand. Just in case.

GROWN-UP ASSISTANT

Kid Chef

GROWN-UPS! Look for this symbol when it's your turn to do something in the recipe. Always supervise kid chefs in the kitchen. Never leave a child unattended.

2. Be clean! Make sure to wash your hands before you start. Baking is a lot of fun, but you won't get to do it very often if you leave a mess behind. If your recipe makes you wait, why not wash some dirty dishes as you go? When you finish baking, clean up everything and put everything away.

3. Be ready! Look over the ingredient list and see if you have everything. If you don't, talk to your assistant to see if you can substitute something else. Also make sure that none of the ingredients will cause an allergic reaction in you or anyone you're baking for.

Using your Tools

This book comes with very helpful baking tools.

HOW TO USE PASTRY BAGS AND PIPING TIPS

1. Cut the tip of a pastry bag about 1 inch (2.5 cm) from the bottom. There are three kinds of piping tips: flat, star, and round. Choose one and place the piping tip into the piping bag.

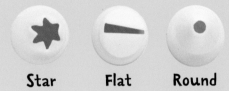

Star   **Flat**   **Round**

2. Use the spatula to fill the pastry bag ¾ full.

3. Twist the wide end closed. You're ready to pipe some frosting like a pro!

HOW TO USE A SPATULA

Use this handy tool to mix, scrape, and fold all your ingredients together. Who will be the lucky person to lick the frosting clean?

HOW TO USE MEASURING SPOONS

Use the back of a knife to "level off" the top of your ingredients.

Just like this.

Not like this.
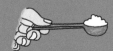

MAKES
1
MUG CAKE

___

⏱
PREP TIME:
5 minutes
BAKE TIME:
1 ½ minutes

GARDEN GNOME
mug cake

GNOME
sweet
GNOME

Truly the most magical recipe in this book. Rich, gooey, chocolatey goodness—ready in under 15 minutes.

YOU WILL NEED

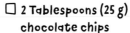

- ☐ 4 Tablespoons (51 g) sugar
- ☐ 3 Tablespoons (38 g) flour
- ☐ 1½ Tablespoons (19.1 g) unsweetened cocoa powder
- ☐ Pinch of salt

- ☐ 2 Tablespoons (25 g) chocolate chips
- ☐ 1½ Tablespoons (22.5 mL) vegetable oil
- ☐ 3½ Tablespoons (51.7 mL) milk

- ☐ ½ teaspoon (2.5 mL) vanilla extract
- ☐ Whipped cream
- ☐ Raspberries
- ☐ Fork
- ☐ Heatproof mug
- ☐ Microwave

1. Place the sugar, flour, cocoa powder, and salt in a heatproof mug. Use a fork to combine together. Stir in chocolate chips.

2. Add the oil, milk, and vanilla extract. Stir together until there are no dry patches.

GROWN-UPS! Do Step 3.

3. Cook the mug in the microwave for 1 minute and 30 seconds. Get your grown-up assistant's help to take it out using oven mitts and set the mug on a heatproof surface.

4. Let it cool for 10 minutes before you dig in. Top your cake with whipped cream and a few raspberries.

TIP Follow instructions on page 13 to make your gnome cake extra special.

PREP TIME:
20 minutes

BAKE TIME:
25–30 minutes

Castle in the Sky
LAYER CAKE

Light-as-a-cloud vanilla cakes float between layers of buttercream frosting, topped with an enchanted castle.

CAKES

YOU WILL NEED

- ☐ 2¼ cups (340 g) flour
- ☐ ½ teaspoon (2 g) salt
- ☐ 3½ teaspoons (15 g) baking powder
- ☐ 1 cup (236 mL) whole milk
- ☐ 1 teaspoon (5 mL) vanilla extract
- ☐ ½ cup (113 g) unsalted butter, softened
- ☐ 1½ cups (301 g) sugar
- ☐ 3 eggs
- ☐ 2 batches Dreamy Butter-Creamy Frosting (pages 14–15)
- ☐ Sprinkles

BAKING TOOLS

- ☐ 2 round 9-inch (23-cm) baking pans
- ☐ Hand mixer (or a whisk with strong arm muscles)
- ☐ Plate or cake stand

GROWN-UPS! Preheat the oven to 350°F (176°C).

1. Prepare your baking pans by greasing them with butter or non-stick spray. Sprinkle a little flour over the pan and shake it to spread the flour evenly.

2. In a medium bowl, combine the dry ingredients: flour, salt, and baking powder. In a small bowl, combine the wet ingredients: milk and vanilla extract.

3. In a large bowl, use a hand mixer or whisk to beat the butter and sugar together until the mixture is light and fluffy. Add eggs, one at a time, and beat until everything looks creamy and pale yellow.

4. On low speed, slowly mix in the dry ingredients a little bit at a time. Then add the wet ingredients. Scrape down the sides of the bowl in between mixing.

GROWN-UPS! Do Step 5 & 6.

5. Divide and pour the batter into the baking pans evenly. Place them in the oven and bake for 25–30 minutes. Have your grown-up assistant use a toothpick and poke the middle of the cakes to check if they're done. If the toothpick comes out clean, the cakes are ready!

6. Remove the pans with oven mitts and let them cool completely on wire racks for 15–20 minutes. Carefully flip each pan over onto a wire rack and gently tap the bottom to release the cakes.

7. While your cakes are cooling, prepare two batches of Dreamy Butter-Creamy Frosting (page 14–15). Once cooled, place one cake on a cake stand. Using a spatula, smooth a thick layer of frosting on top. Take the second cake and place it upside down on top of the first cake. Frost the rest of the cake starting from the top and working your way down the sides.

8. Decorate the cake with sprinkles and cake toppers.

Decorations

Here are a couple ways to craft some fun decorations to make your treats extra magical.

YOU WILL NEED

- ☐ Punch-out sheet
- ☐ Sticker sheet
- ☐ Toothpicks
- ☐ Baker's twine
- ☐ Paper straws
- ☐ Tape
- ☐ Scissors

Toppers

1. Punch-out a paper shape from the punch-out sheet.

2. Attach the paper shape to a toothpick with a small piece of tape.

Banners

1. Using scissors, cut a string of baker's twine about 6 inches (15 cm) long.

2. Fold some rectangular stickers over the baker's twine. You can use a marker to draw decorations or letters.

3. Cut a slit near the top of two straws. Wrap each end of baker's twine around the slits.

MAKES
**2 ½
CUPS**
(591 ML)

PREP TIME:
5 minutes

MAKE TIME:
5 minutes

Dreamy Butter-Creamy FROSTING

Once you've mastered whipping up this icing, you can use it in all the other cake recipes in this book!

CAKES

YOU WILL NEED

- ☐ 1 cup (227 g) unsalted butter, softened
- ☐ 3½ cups (703 g) powdered sugar
- ☐ 1 teaspoon (5 mL) vanilla extract
- ☐ 1-2 Tablespoons (15-30 mL) milk

- ☐ Medium bowl
- ☐ Hand mixer (or a whisk with strong arm muscles)
- ☐ Spatula

1. Beat the butter in a bowl on medium speed until it's smooth.

2. Slowly add the powdered sugar a little bit at a time and mix on low speed. Scrape down the sides of the bowl in between mixing.

3. Add the vanilla extract and milk. Mix the frosting on medium speed until it's smooth and creamy. Use a spatula to spread frosting or see instructions on page 7 to fill a pastry bag for decorating.

TIP To make colored frosting, add a few drops of food coloring!

MAKES
24
DONUTS

PREP TIME:
20 minutes
BAKE TIME:
18–20 minutes

coconut YETI DONUTS

Grrr! These frosted donuts bite back! Try popping one in the freezer for a chilly treat.

YOU WILL NEED

- ☐ Cake batter (page 10–12)
- ☐ Dreamy Butter-Creamy Frosting (page 14–15)
- ☐ Blue food coloring
- ☐ 2 cups (256 g) shredded coconut
- ☐ 48 almonds
- ☐ 96 yellow chocolate candies
- ☐ 48 candy eyes
- ☐ Spoon
- ☐ Donut pan
- ☐ Non-stick spray

GROWN-UPS! Preheat the oven to 350°F (176°C).

GROWN-UPS! Do Step 2.

1. Follow the recipe on pages 10–12 to prepare the batter. Grease the donut pan with non-stick spray. Carefully spoon the batter into the donut pan, filling the cups halfway.

2. Bake the donuts for 18–20 minutes. Remove the pan with oven mitts and let cool on a wire rack for 15 minutes. Use a toothpick and poke the middle of the donuts to check if they're done. If the toothpick comes out clean, they're ready! Carefully remove the donuts from the pan and let them cool completely.

3. While the donuts are cooling, prepare the Dreamy Butter-Creamy Frosting (page 14–15). Add a drop of blue food coloring to the frosting and mix with a spatula. Spread frosting on a donut. Place the shredded coconut in a bowl. Then dip each donut frosting side down into the coconut.

4. To add horns, stick two almonds on top of the head. Add candy eyes under the horns. Stick four yellow chocolate candies inside the top half of the donut hole for teeth.

TIP If you don't have a donut mold, use a cupcake tin to make yeti cupcakes instead!

17

MAKES
24
CUPCAKES

PREP TIME:
20 minutes
BAKE TIME:
18–20 minutes

mystery surprise
Cupcakes

Sure, they might look like ordinary, yet
oh-so-delicious cupcakes on the outside.
But inside, they hold a secret.
(Spoiler alert: The secret is sprinkles.)

YOU WILL NEED

- ☐ Cake batter (pages 10–12)
- ☐ Dreamy Butter-Creamy Frosting (pages 14–15)
- ☐ Sprinkles
- ☐ Sanding sugar
- ☐ Cupcake liners
- ☐ Cupcake tin
- ☐ Teaspoon

GROWN-UPS! Preheat the oven to 350°F (176°C).

1. Follow the recipe on pages 10–12 to make the batter. Prepare the cupcake tin with cupcake liners. Carefully spoon the cake batter into the liners and fill each cup halfway.

2. Bake the cupcakes for 18–20 minutes. Remove the tin with oven mitts and cool on a wire rack for 15 minutes. Carefully remove the cupcakes from the tin and let them cool completely.

GROWN-UPS! Do Step 2.

3. While the cupcakes are cooling, prepare the Dreamy Butter-Creamy Frosting (pages 14–15). Use a teaspoon and carefully scoop out a small hole in the middle of the cupcake. Make sure not to go all the way to the bottom! Fill the hole with sprinkles. Place the scooped-out piece of cupcake back on top of the hole.

4. Frost the cupcake with a spatula or spoon and decorate with more sprinkles and sanding sugar.

BAKING CHALLENGE For swirly decoration, follow instructions on page 5 to pipe the frosting onto the cupcake. Start from the outside and slowly squeeze the frosting in a circular motion until you reach the center. Voilà!

MAKES
40
TRUFFLES

PREP TIME:
50 minutes
BAKE TIME:
20 minutes

Crystal Cake
TRUFFLES

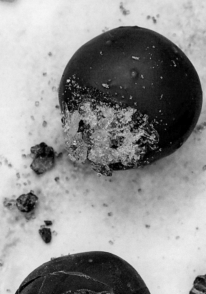

Inspired by geodes, these
mystical-looking crystals are
actually cake, dunked in a
candy coating.

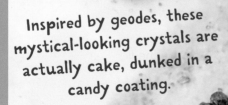

YOU WILL NEED

- ☐ 1 cake (page 10–12)
- ☐ Dreamy Butter-Creamy Frosting (page 14–15)
- ☐ 1 cup (125 g) chocolate candy melts
- ☐ 1 Tablespoon (15 mL) coconut oil
- ☐ 30 pieces of hard candy
- ☐ Sanding sugar
- ☐ Heatproof bowl
- ☐ Fork
- ☐ Wax paper
- ☐ Rolling pin
- ☐ Plastic bag

1. In a large bowl, use your (clean) hands to crumble up the cake. Add 2 cups (473 mL) of frosting. Use a spatula to mix the cake and frosting together.

2. Use a Tablespoon to scoop out a heaping spoonful of cake mixture. Use your hands to roll the mixture into a cake ball. Arrange neatly on a baking sheet on top of wax paper. Freeze the cake balls for 10–15 minutes.

3. Meanwhile, in a heatproof bowl, have your grown-up assistant melt chocolate candy melts and coconut oil in a microwave in 15-second bursts until smooth. Use a spatula to stir in between.

GROWN-UPS! Do Step 4.

4. Line a baking sheet with wax paper. One at a time, drop each chilled cake ball into the candy melt and push it around with a fork to coat the cake. Lift it out and gently shake the cake to let any excess candy melt drip off. Place them on the wax paper.

5. Place some hard candies in a plastic bag. Use a rolling pin to crush the candy into small chunks.

6. Spoon a little bit of candy melt on the flat side of a cake ball. Sprinkle with sanding sugar and press the crushed candy bits in the center.

MAKES
24
COOKIES

PREP TIME:
45 minutes

BAKE TIME:
6–8 minutes

Pixie Dust
sugar
COOKIES

Sprinkle a simple cookie recipe with magic! Any colorful sugar you have on hand is perfect.

YOU WILL NEED

- ☐ 2¾ cups (374 g) flour
- ☐ 2 teaspoons (8.5 g) cream of tartar
- ☐ 1 teaspoon (4.2 g) baking soda
- ☐ ½ teaspoon (2 g) salt

- ☐ ¾ cup (170 g) unsalted butter, softened
- ☐ 1½ cups (301 g) sugar
- ☐ 2 eggs

- ☐ 1½ teaspoons (7.5 mL) vanilla extract
- ☐ Sanding sugar in your favorite colors
- ☐ Hand mixer or spatula with strong arm muscles
- ☐ Plate

GROWN-UPS! Preheat the oven to 400°F (204°C).

1. Line a baking sheet with parchment paper. Pour sanding sugar onto a plate and set it aside.

2. In a medium bowl, combine flour, cream of tartar, baking soda, and salt.

3. In another bowl, mix the butter and sugar with a hand mixer until they are light and fluffy. Add the eggs one at a time, mixing in between. Add the vanilla extract. Scrape down the sides of the bowl and mix until everything is combined.

GROWN-UPS! Do Step 5.

4. Add the dry ingredients from Step 2 and mix until they are combined. Scoop 1 Tablespoon (13 g) of cookie dough and roll it into a ball. Gently roll each ball in the sanding sugar and place them on the baking sheet.

5. Bake the cookies for 6–8 minutes. Remove the cookies from the oven with oven mitts and let them cool for a few minutes. Transfer the cookies onto a wire rack to cool for 10 more minutes.

MAKES
24
COOKIES

PREP TIME:
30 minutes

BAKE TIME:
13–15 minutes

BIG FOOT cookies

How else could those footprints get there? It must be the work of the legendary, forest-dwelling Big Foot!

YOU WILL NEED

- ☐ 2 cups (272 g) flour
- ☐ ½ teaspoon (2 g) baking powder
- ☐ Pinch of salt
- ☐ 1 cup (201 g) sugar

- ☐ ½ cup (113 g) unsalted butter, softened
- ☐ 1 teaspoon (5 mL) vanilla extract
- ☐ 2 eggs

- ☐ 24 chocolate chips
- ☐ 72 mini chocolate chips
- ☐ 24 chocolate candy melts
- ☐ Hand mixer (or spatula with strong arm muscles)

GROWN-UPS! Preheat the oven to 325°F (162°C).

1. Line the baking sheet with parchment paper. In a large bowl, combine flour, baking powder, and salt.

2. Mix the sugar and butter with a hand mixer until they are light and fluffy. Beat in the vanilla and eggs.

3. Slowly add the dry ingredients from Step 1 to the wet ingredients from Step 2 and mix until they are combined.

4. Scoop 1½ Tablespoons (22 g) of dough and roll into an oblong ball. Press it slightly with the palm of your hand. Add a chocolate candy melt in the middle for the pad, a chocolate chip for the big toe, and three mini chocolate chips for small toes. Arrange neatly on a baking sheet.

GROWN-UPS! Do Step 5.

5. Bake for 13–15 minutes. Remove baking sheet from the oven with oven mitts and let cool for a couple minutes. Transfer cookies onto a wire rack and cool for 10 more minutes.

MAKES
18
SANDWICHES

PREP TIME:
10 minutes

BAKE TIME:
10–12 minutes

Unicorn
SANDWICHES

If you find a herd of unicorns in the wild, they might ask you to make a batch of their favorite snack.

YOU WILL NEED

- [ ] 1½ cups (204 g) flour
- [ ] ⅔ cup (134 g) sugar
- [ ] ½ teaspoon (2 g) baking soda
- [ ] ¼ teaspoon (1 g) salt
- [ ] ¼ cup (59 mL) vegetable oil

- [ ] 1 egg
- [ ] ½ cup (118 mL) buttermilk
- [ ] 1 teaspoon (5 mL) vanilla extract
- [ ] Sprinkles
- [ ] Sanding sugar in your favorite colors

- [ ] Dreamy Butter-Creamy Frosting (pages 14–15)
- [ ] Spoon
- [ ] Hand mixer (or whisk with strong arm muscles)

✳ GROWN-UPS! Preheat the oven to 350°F (176°C).

1. Line a baking sheet with parchment paper. In a large bowl, whisk together the flour, sugar, baking soda, and salt. In a small bowl, whisk together the vegetable oil, egg, buttermilk, and vanilla.

2. Combine the wet ingredients into the dry ingredients and mix with a hand mixer until they are combined. The mixture will look sticky and squishy.

3. Neatly scoop a spoonful of batter on the baking sheet. Try to make them as round as possible. Top each scoop with sprinkles.

✳ GROWN-UPS! Do Step 4.

4. Bake the cookies for 10–12 minutes. Remove the pan with oven mitts and allow the cookies to cool on the sheet for 2 minutes. Transfer the cookies onto a wire rack to cool completely.

5. Using a spatula, spoon some Dreamy Butter-Creamy Frosting (pages 14–15) onto the flat side of a cookie. Gently place another cookie flat side down on top of the frosting. Roll the frosting edge of the cookie in some sanding sugar.

MAKES
72
COOKIES

PREP TIME:
45 minutes
BAKE TIME:
12–15 minutes

RAINBOW COOKIES

COOKIES

Ready for a challenge? If you feel like a master chef, try your hand at these slice-and-bake rainbows.

FOLLOW THIS CHART TO MIX IN YOUR COLORS:

- 2 cups (249 g) dough + 10 drops red
- 1⅓ cups (181 g) dough + 2 drops red + 10 drops yellow
- 1¼ cups (119 g) dough + 10 drops yellow
- ⅓ cup (79 g) dough + 10 drops yellow + 2 drops blue
- ½ cup (62 g) dough + 10 drops blue
- ¼ cup (36 g) dough + 8 drops red + 3 drops blue

YOU WILL NEED

- ☐ 2 cups (272 g) flour
- ☐ ½ teaspoon (2 g) baking powder
- ☐ Pinch of salt
- ☐ ⅔ cup (134 g) powdered sugar
- ☐ ¼ cup (50 g) sugar
- ☐ 1¼ cup (284 g) butter, cold and diced
- ☐ 1 teaspoon (5 mL) vanilla extract
- ☐ Food coloring in red, yellow, and blue
- ☐ Hand mixer
- ☐ Plastic wrap
- ☐ Rolling pin
- ☐ Knife

1. In a medium bowl, combine flour, baking powder, salt, powdered sugar, and sugar. Add cold butter and mix until the mixture is crumbly. Add vanilla and mix until a dough ball forms.

2. Follow the chart on page 28 to divide the dough and use food coloring to mix in the colors.

3. Sprinkle some powdered sugar onto your work surface. Roll out the purple dough into a fat snake, about 10 inches (25.5 cm) long.

GROWN-UPS! Preheat the oven to 325°F (162°C).

GROWN-UPS! Do Step 6.

4. Use a rolling pin to roll out the blue dough ¼ inch (6 mm) thick. Place the purple dough on top of the blue dough and gently roll together. Pinch the seams closed. If the dough cracks, pinch tears together and gently smooth out the dough. It's OK if a few cracks remain.

5. Repeat Step 4 with the remaining colors in this order: green, yellow, orange, and red. Wrap the rainbow log in plastic wrap and freeze for 30 minutes.

6. Line a baking sheet with parchment paper. Slice the rainbow log into ¼ inch (6 mm) thick pieces. Then cut each cookie in half to make two rainbows. Arrange the rainbows neatly on the baking sheet. Bake for 12–15 minutes. Remove the sheet from the oven with oven mitts and let the cookies cool on a wire rack for 10 minutes.

CHOCOLATE

Magic wand
PRETZELS

Wave an ordinary pretzel in a cauldron of chocolate ... Tada! You are now the proud owner of a magic wand!

YOU WILL NEED

- ☐ 6 Tablespoons (129 g) peanut butter
- ☐ ¼ cup (50 g) powdered sugar
- ☐ 20 pretzel rods
- ☐ 1½ cups (192 g) chocolate candy melts
- ☐ 4 Tablespoons (60 mL) coconut oil
- ☐ Sprinkles
- ☐ Tall heatproof cup
- ☐ Wax paper

1. Mix the peanut butter and powdered sugar together. Use the round piping tip and follow instructions on page 5 to fill a pastry bag with the peanut butter mixture.

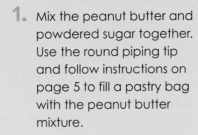

2. Line a baking sheet with wax paper. Arrange the pretzel sticks neatly in a row. Pipe the peanut butter on top of each pretzel rod in a zigzag pattern. Leave space at the bottom! Freeze the pretzels for 15 minutes until the peanut butter is firm.

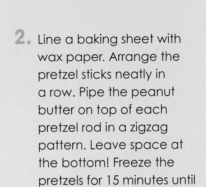

GROWN-UPS! Do Step 3.

3. Add the chocolate candy melts and coconut oil in a tall heatproof cup. Melt the candy melts in 15-second bursts until it has melted. Stir well in between melting.

4. Dip each pretzel rod into the candy melt. Tip the cup slightly and roll each pretzel so it's totally covered. Gently shake off the extra chocolate.

5. Decorate the wands with sprinkles.

TIP You can use white chocolate to make white wands!

CHOCOLATE

GIANT
MONSTER
CLAWS

RAWR!

Hungry monsters will want
to get their claws on these
chocolate-dipped apples.

YOU WILL NEED

- [ ] 6 apple slices
- [ ] ½ cup (64 g) chocolate chips
- [ ] Toppings of your choice: shredded coconut, chopped peanuts or banana chips, raisins, or granola
- [ ] Heatproof bowl
- [ ] Baking sheet
- [ ] Parchment paper

GROWN-UPS!
Do Step 2.

1. Place parchment paper on a baking sheet.

2. Add the chocolate chips in a heatproof bowl. Microwave the bowl in 15-second bursts until the chocolate has melted, stirring in between. Remove the bowl using oven mitts.

3. Carefully dip each apple slice halfway into the chocolate. Sprinkle the chocolate with your favorite topping: coconut, peanuts, banana chips, raisins, or granola. Arrange the slices neatly on the baking sheet and let the chocolate cool.

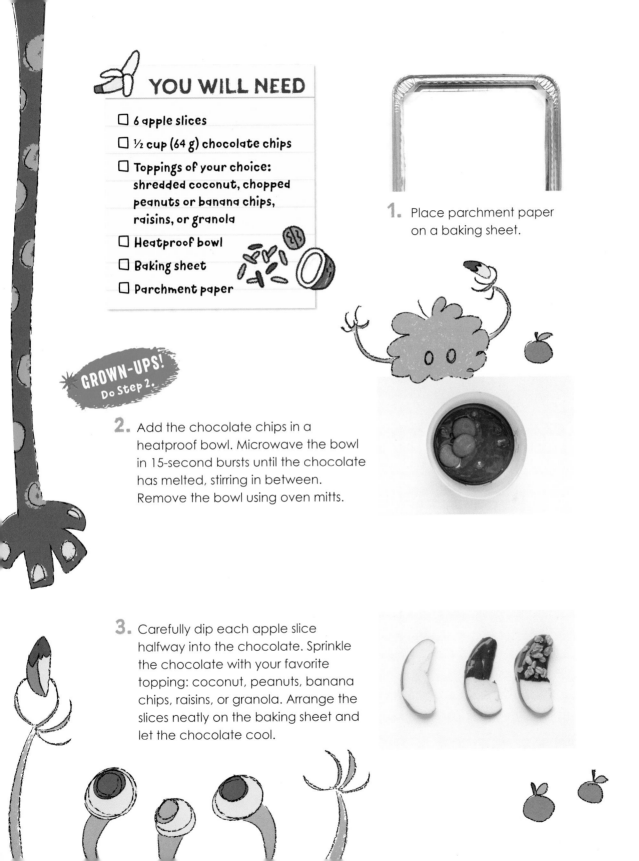

MAKES
4
CUPS

PREP TIME:
10 minutes

MAKE TIME:
30 minutes

treasure treats mix

CHOCOLATE

Any kind of chocolate will be delicious and make enough to feed a crowd of treasure-hunting pirates.

YOU WILL NEED

- ☐ ½ cup (64 g) pink candy melts
- ☐ ½ cup (64 g) blue candy melts
- ☐ ½ cup (64 g) purple candy melts
- ☐ ½ cup (64 g) yellow candy melts
- ☐ 2 Tablespoons (30 mL) coconut oil
- ☐ 1⅓ cups (156 g) powdered sugar
- ☐ 4 cups (512 g) toasted rice square cereal
- ☐ Spoon
- ☐ Heatproof bowl
- ☐ 4 large plastic bags

1. Combine the pink candy melts and ½ Tablespoon (7.5 mL) of coconut oil in a heatproof bowl.

2. Microwave the bowl for 15 seconds. Use oven mitts to remove the bowl and stir with a spoon. Keep microwaving in 15-second intervals until the candy melts have liquefied.

3. Add the melted candy and 1 cup of toasted rice square cereal into a plastic bag. Gently toss the bag to coat the cereal. Add ⅓ cup (39 g) powdered sugar and gently toss the bag again. Pour the cereal onto a baking tray and let it sit for 5–10 minutes to dry.

4. Repeat Steps 1–3 with the other three colors of candy melts. Pour the dried treasure into a large bowl and mix.

MAKES
12
WISHING
STARS

⏱

PREP TIME:
10 minutes
MAKE TIME:
30 minutes

MARSHMALLOW
wishing
stars

CHOCOLATE

If you wished for
a crispy, crunchy,
ooey, gooey treat,
then guess what?
Your wish just
came true!

YOU WILL NEED

- ☐ 3 Tablespoons (45 g) unsalted butter
- ☐ 4 cups (512 g) mini marshmallows
- ☐ 6 cups (768 g) puffed rice cereal
- ☐ Assorted sprinkles
- ☐ Non-stick spray
- ☐ Star shape cookie cutter
- ☐ Large bowl
- ☐ Saucepan

1. Spritz a large bowl and baking tray with non-stick spray. Place the puffed rice cereal into the bowl.

GROWN-UPS!
Do Step 2.

2. Melt the butter in a saucepan over low heat. Add the marshmallows and stir until they are completely melted. Pour the melted marshmallows into the cereal, then stir until the cereal is evenly coated.

3. Pour the cereal mixture onto the baking tray and press the mixture down evenly with a spatula. Add sprinkles on top and press them down. Allow the cereal to cool for 5 minutes.

4. Cut out stars with a cookie cutter.

TIP To make your star extra sweet, drizzle some melted chocolate on top!

—

PREP TIME:
20 minutes

BAKE TIME:
8–10 minutes

DRAGON SCALE

tortilla CHIPS

BREADS

Oven-baked chips taste great
with fire-breathing salsa . . .
Or mild-breathing salsa if you're
a peaceful dragon.

YOU WILL NEED

- ☐ 6 spinach tortillas
- ☐ 6 Tablespoons (90 mL) olive oil
- ☐ 4 tomatoes, diced
- ☐ 1 onion, diced
- ☐ ½ cup (64 g) cilantro, chopped
- ☐ 3 garlic cloves, minced
- ☐ 1 Tablespoon (15 mL) lime juice
- ☐ Salt and pepper
- ☐ Pizza cutter or kitchen scissors
- ☐ Pastry brush

GROWN-UPS!
Preheat the oven to 350°F (176°C).

1. Using a pizza cutter or kitchen scissors, cut each tortilla into eight slices.

2. Coat each tortilla on both sides with olive oil using a pastry brush. Arrange the tortillas neatly on a baking sheet.

GROWN-UPS!
Do Step 3.

3. Bake the chips for 8–10 minutes. Remove the pan from the oven with oven mitts and place the chips in a bowl.

4. While the chips are baking, combine tomatoes, onion, cilantro, garlic, and lime juice in a medium bowl. Add salt and pepper to taste.

TIP Try using different kinds of tortillas for a variety of dragon scales: tomato tortillas for red dragons, or corn tortillas for golden dragons.

MAKES
4-6
SERVINGS

ACTIVE TIME:
15 minutes

INACTIVE TIME:
1 hour

ABRACADABRA DOUGH

No dough in the fridge? Well, with a few simple ingredients—presto! You can make it yourself.

YOU WILL NEED

- ☐ ¼ oz (7 g) packet dry yeast
- ☐ 1 teaspoon (4 g) sugar
- ☐ ¾ cup (180 mL) warm water
- ☐ 2½ cups (350 g) flour, plus a little extra
- ☐ ½ teaspoon (1 g) salt
- ☐ 2 Tablespoons (30 mL) vegetable oil
- ☐ Mixing bowl
- ☐ Mixing spoon
- ☐ Clean kitchen towel

1. Put the yeast and sugar in the mixing bowl with the warm water and let them sit for 5 minutes until the mixture looks foamy.

2. Add the flour, salt, and oil to the bowl. Mix everything together.

3. Turn the dough onto a lightly floured surface. Turn the dough over and over, pressing the palm of your hand into the center of the dough, then folding the sides into the middle. This is called kneading. Do this about 100 times. You can do it!

4. Place the dough in a bowl, cover it with a towel, and let it rise in a warm, dry place about 1 hour until it doubles in size.

5. Ta da! You just made pizza dough. Go ahead and follow the instructions on the next page to finish making your pizza.

MAKES
4
KRAKENS

PREP TIME:
20 minutes

BAKE TIME:
10 minutes

KRAKEN PIZZA

Unleash this adorable sea
monster from your oven.
Krakens love parties, so make
these pizzas with friends!

YOU WILL NEED

- [ ] **Abracadabra Dough** (page 40–41)
- [ ] **2 cups (473 mL) pizza sauce**
- [ ] **¼ cup (32 g) flour**
- [ ] **2 cups (256 g) mozzarella cheese, shredded**
- [ ] **8 pepperonis**
- [ ] **Butter knife**
- [ ] **Olives, sliced**
- [ ] **Kitchen scissors**
- [ ] **Rolling pin**
- [ ] **Spoon**

GROWN-UPS! Preheat the oven to 400°F (204°C).

1. Line a baking sheet with a sheet of parchment paper. Use a butter knife to cut the pizza dough into quarters. Sprinkle your work surface with a little flour. Roll the dough into an oblong shape with a rolling pin and transfer onto the baking sheet. Use kitchen scissors to cut some tentacles.

TIP It's best if the pizza dough is at room temperature when you roll it.

2. Spoon some pizza sauce onto the body and tentacles of the kraken. Then sprinkle it with mozzarella cheese. Add two pepperonis for eyes and two olives for pupils. Place olives on the tentacles for suction cups.

TIP You can use a variety of toppings to create different faces: Peppers, mushrooms, onions, even anchovies!

3. Bake the krakens for 10 minutes. Remove them from the oven using oven mitts and serve.

MAKES
1
POT

PREP TIME:
20 minutes
BAKE TIME:
18–20 minutes

BREADS

POT o' GOLD
cheesy bread

If the end of the rainbow seems too far away, make your own leprechaun gold. Perfect with tomato soup!

YOU WILL NEED

- ☐ Abracadabra Dough (pages 40–41)
- ☐ 4 garlic cloves, minced
- ☐ 1 cup (128 g) broccoli, shredded
- ☐ 1½ cups (192 g) cheddar cheese, shredded
- ☐ 2 Tablespoons butter, melted
- ☐ 8-inch (20.5 cm) cast-iron skillet (or cake pan)
- ☐ Pastry brush

GROWN-UPS! Preheat the oven to 375°F (190°C).

1. Grease the skillet with butter. Cut the dough in half. Then half again (and again and again!) until you have 16 pieces.

2. Combine garlic, broccoli, and 1 cup (64 g) of cheddar cheese in a bowl.

GROWN-UPS! Do Step 4 & 5.

3. Slightly flatten a piece of dough. Place a Tablespoon of broccoli cheddar mixture in the middle and wrap up the dough like a dumpling. Pinch the ends closed. Place each roll with the seam side down into the skillet.

4. Brush the top of the rolls with melted butter. Sprinkle the remaining shredded cheese over the top.

5. Bake the rolls for 18–20 minutes until golden brown.

MAKES
9
ROLLS

PREP TIME:
20 minutes
BAKE TIME:
28–30 minutes

Hypnotic Cinna-Swirl Rolls

Spellbinding layers of fluffy
dough and cinnamon may make
you feel sleepy... very sleepy...

YOU WILL NEED

- ☐ Abracadabra Dough (page 40-41)
- ☐ ¼ cup (57 g) unsalted butter, melted
- ☐ 2 Tablespoons (25 g) cinnamon
- ☐ 1 cup (201 g) sugar
- ☐ 1 Tablespoon (15 mL) water
- ☐ Non-stick spray
- ☐ Serrated knife
- ☐ Pastry brush
- ☐ 8 x 8 in (20 x 20 cm) square baking pan

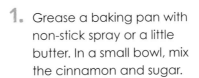

GROWN-UPS!
Preheat the oven to 375°F (190°C).

1. Grease a baking pan with non-stick spray or a little butter. In a small bowl, mix the cinnamon and sugar.

2. Roll out the dough on a lightly floured surface into a ½-inch (13-mm) thick rectangle. Brush the melted butter on top. Sprinkle evenly with the cinnamon-and-sugar mixture.

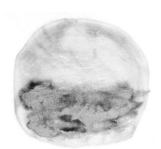

GROWN-UPS!
Do Step 3.

3. Gently pick up the long edge and roll the dough into a spiral. You'll end up with a long cinnamon log! Using a serrated knife, slice the dough about 1½ (4 cm) inches thick.

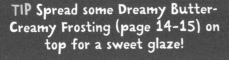

TIP Spread some Dreamy Butter-Creamy Frosting (page 14-15) on top for a sweet glaze!

4. Transfer the rolls onto the baking pan with a little space in between. Brush the rolls with the rest of the melted butter.

GROWN-UPS! Do Step 5.

5. Bake for 28–30 minutes. Remove the pan from the oven with oven mitts and let the rolls cool for 15 minutes.

MAKES
18
CHEESECAKES

PREP TIME:
30 minutes

CHILL TIME:
4–6 hours
or overnight

NO-BAKE *Fairy* cheesecake

One of these mini cakes is
the perfect size for a party
of fairies—or one of you!

YOU WILL NEED

- ☐ 1½ cups (192 g) graham cracker crumbs
- ☐ ¼ cup (55 g) brown sugar
- ☐ ½ teaspoon (2 g) cinnamon
- ☐ Pinch of salt
- ☐ ½ cup (113 g) unsalted butter, melted
- ☐ 16 ounces (453 g) cream cheese, softened
- ☐ ½ cup (100 g) powdered sugar
- ☐ 1⅓ cups (330 mL) heavy cream
- ☐ 1 Tablespoon (15 mL) lemon juice
- ☐ 1 teaspoon (5 mL) vanilla extract
- ☐ ½ pint of your favorite berries
- ☐ Hand mixer
- ☐ Mini cupcake tin
- ☐ Plastic knife

GROWN-UPS! Do Step 1.

TIP You can make graham cracker crumbs by placing graham crackers in a plastic storage bag and crushing them with a rolling pin.

1. In a large bowl, combine the graham cracker crumbs, brown sugar, cinnamon, salt, and melted butter. Stir until the mixture clumps together like wet sand.

2. Grease the mini cupcake tin with some butter. Fill the space ¼ of the way up with graham cracker mix. Use your fingers to press down firmly.

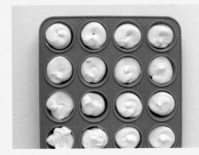

3. In a large bowl, use a hand mixer to beat the cream cheese and powdered sugar until they are smooth. Add the cream a little at a time mixing in between. Scrape down the sides of the bowl. Stir in the lemon juice and vanilla.

4. Fill each cupcake with cream-cheese filling. Chill them overnight. Carefully run a plastic knife around the edge of the cheesecake to remove from the cupcake tin. Top each cake with your favorite berries.

TIP Follow instructions on page 13 to make little fairies flying above the cheesecakes!

49

Mermaid Sand Dollar HAND PIES

Flaky, crispy hand pies—
no fork needed! Any kind of jam
would be equally delicious.

YOU WILL NEED

- ☐ 2 sheets of pie crust, thawed
- ☐ ½ cup (170 g) blueberry jam
- ☐ Egg
- ☐ 2 Tablespoons (29 mL) water
- ☐ 3 Tablespoons (37.5 g) coarse sugar
- ☐ 3-inch (7.5-cm) round cookie cutter or jar lid
- ☐ Rolling pin
- ☐ Pastry brush
- ☐ Fork
- ☐ Butter knife

GROWN-UPS! Preheat the oven to 425°F (218°C).

1. Line the baking sheet with parchment paper. Use a cookie cutter to cut out 16 circles from the pie crust. You can gather the scraps and use a rolling pin to roll out more dough. Arrange eight of the circles on the cookie sheet.

2. Place ½ Tablespoon (7.5 mL) of blueberry jam in the middle of each circle. Whisk the egg and water to make "egg wash." Dip a pastry brush into the egg wash, and paint the edges of each circle of pie crust.

3. Place another circle on top of each crust, over the jam. Use a fork to press down the edges around the pies. Then use a butter knife to cut four slits around the center.

GROWN-UPS! Do Step 5.

4. Brush the tops with more egg wash and sprinkle over with coarse sugar.

5. Bake the pies for 12–15 minutes. Remove the pan from the oven using oven mitts and let the pies cool for 10 minutes.

BAKING CHALLENGE To make a shimmery glaze, mix together 2 cups (272 g) of powdered sugar with 3 Tablespoons (44 mL) of milk or water. Drizzle glaze on top of the pies and top with sprinkles.

MAKES
9
PASTRIES

PREP TIME:
10 minutes

BAKE TIME:
10–15 minutes

POOF!
Pastry

Put a plate of these
out for your friends,
and they will disappear
right before your eyes!

YOU WILL NEED

- ☐ 1 sheet puff pastry, thawed
- ☐ 8 oz (224 g) Brie cheese, cut into 12 cubes
- ☐ 1 cup (340 g) raspberry jam
- ☐ Egg
- ☐ Pastry brush
- ☐ Pizza cutter or kitchen scissors
- ☐ Cupcake tin

GROWN-UPS!
Preheat the oven to 375°F (190°C).

1. Cut puff pastry sheets into 3 x 3 inch (7.5 x 7.5 cm) squares with a pizza cutter. Place each square into the cupcake tin.

2. Place a piece of Brie in the middle of each pastry. Dollop a little raspberry jam on top. Mix an egg with 2 Tablespoons (30 mL) of water to make "egg wash." Use a pastry brush to coat the top of the crusts with the egg wash.

GROWN-UPS! Do Step 3.

3. Bake for 10–15 minutes. Remove the pan from the oven with oven mitts and let cool for 5 minutes.

MAKES
12
QUICHES

—

PREP TIME:
15 minutes

BAKE TIME:
25–30 minutes

SWAMP MONSTER QUICHES

Look carefully, and you might spot a strange creature swimming in your brunch!

YOU WILL NEED

- [ ] 2 sheets of pie crust, thawed
- [ ] 1 cup (128 g) Swiss cheese, grated
- [ ] 1 cup (128 g) spinach, chopped
- [ ] 1 Tablespoon (15 g) red bell pepper, diced
- [ ] 4 eggs
- [ ] ½ cup (125 mL) milk
- [ ] ½ teaspoon (2 g) salt
- [ ] 4-inch (10-cm) round cookie cutter
- [ ] Non-stick spray
- [ ] Cupcake tin
- [ ] Whisk

GROWN-UPS!
Preheat the oven to 375°F (190°C).

1. Spray the cupake tin with non-stick spray. Use a cookie cutter to cut out circles from the pie crust. You can gather the scraps and use a rolling pin to roll out more dough. Press the pie crust into each space of the cupcake tin.

2. In a medium bowl, whisk together the cheese, spinach, red pepper, eggs, milk, and salt.

3. Pour the egg mixture into each crust, leaving ¼ inch (6 mm) on top.

GROWN-UPS!
Do Step 4.

4. Bake the quiches for 25–30 minutes. Remove the pan from the oven using oven mitts and let them cool for 5 minutes. Serve warm.

TIP Follow instructions on page 13 to make a monster emerging from the swamp!

MAKES
2
SHAKES

🕐

PREP TIME:
10 minutes

MAKE TIME:
10 minutes

Dream Shake

Over-the-top candy-coated milkshakes...this is what dreams are made of!

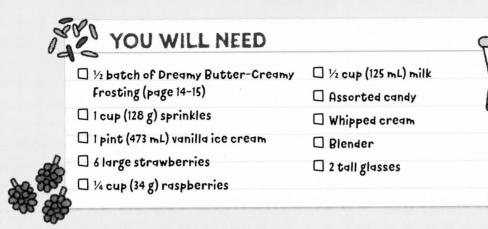

YOU WILL NEED

- ☐ ½ batch of Dreamy Butter-Creamy Frosting (page 14-15)
- ☐ 1 cup (128 g) sprinkles
- ☐ 1 pint (473 mL) vanilla ice cream
- ☐ 6 large strawberries
- ☐ ¼ cup (34 g) raspberries
- ☐ ½ cup (125 mL) milk
- ☐ Assorted candy
- ☐ Whipped cream
- ☐ Blender
- ☐ 2 tall glasses

GROWN-UPS! Do Step 2.

1. Spread frosting around the outside rim of each glass. Roll the frosting in sprinkles.

2. Place the ice cream, strawberries, raspberries, and milk into the blender. Blend them until they are smooth.

3. Pour the milkshake into the prepared glasses. Top each shake with whipped cream, sprinkles, and candy.

TIP To make magical toppers, punch-out the unicorns from the punch-out sheet and poke a gold straw through the slits. Other recipes that make fun toppings include the Treasure Treats Mix (pages 34-35), Magic Wand Pretzels (pages 30-31), and Marshmallow Wishing Stars (pages 36-37).

MAKES
1
PUDDING

—

🕐

PREP TIME:
5 minutes

CHILL TIME:
2 hours

Twilight Chia Seed Pudding

Twilight means you can eat
it early in the morning...
or add sprinkles to make it
an evening time dessert!

POTIONS

YOU WILL NEED

- ☐ ¼ cup (32 g) blueberries plus a little extra
- ☐ 1 cup (250 mL) milk
- ☐ Pinch of cinnamon
- ☐ 2 teaspoons (10 mL) maple syrup
- ☐ ⅓ cup (43 g) chia seeds
- ☐ ¼ cup (32 g) granola

- ☐ Sprinkles
- ☐ Blender
- ☐ Whisk
- ☐ Small bowl
- ☐ Plastic wrap
- ☐ Small cup or jar

GROWN-UPS! Do Step 1.

1. Blend the blueberries, milk, cinnamon, and maple syrup together.

2. Place the blueberry milk into a bowl. Add chia seeds and mix it with a whisk. Cover the bowl with plastic wrap and place it in the refrigerator for 2 hours.

3. Spoon some chia seed pudding into a small cup. Top your masterpiece with extra blueberries, granola, or sprinkles.

Credits

EDITOR: Gina Kim

DESIGNERS: Meghan Templehof and Vanessa Han

DOODLE ILLUSTRATOR: Reese Walker and Lizzy Doyle

PHOTOGRAPHER: Alexandra Grablewski

FOOD STYLIST: Chris Barsch

BUYERS: Roxy Leung and Jacob Kessler

PACKAGE DESIGNER: Owen Keating

SAFETY MANAGERS: Sam Walker and Karen Fuchs

SPECIAL THANKS: Stacy Lellos, Netta Rabin, Caitlin Harpin, Liz Shim, and Hannah Rogge

Get creative with more from KLUTZ

Looking for more goof-proof activities, sneak peeks, and giveaways? Find us online!

 KlutzCertified   KlutzCertified   KlutzCertified   KlutzCertified   Klutz

Klutz.com • thefolks@klutz.com • 1-800-737-4123